Original title:
Ocean Waters, Island Breezes

Copyright © 2025 Creative Arts Management OÜ
All rights reserved.

Author: Dante Kingsley
ISBN HARDBACK: 978-1-80581-696-6
ISBN PAPERBACK: 978-1-80581-223-4
ISBN EBOOK: 978-1-80581-696-6

Reflections on the Tide

A crab tells jokes with its claws,
While seagulls squawk with no pause.
The fish swim by in tiny schools,
Pretending they're all ocean fools.

The wave curls up and starts to grin,
Announcing that the fun begins!
Kids splash about, giggles abound,
While dad just searches for his drowned crown.

Breezy Elysium

A kite decides to take a dive,
As beach balls bounce and tumble live.
The sunscreen flies—a slippery mess,
While sandcastles fail at their best.

Towels whip like flags in a match,
Sandy sandwiches make quite a catch.
Breezes tickle every nose,
And we laugh at all our sandy woes.

Surfing the Celestial Foam

A dolphin slips and slides with glee,
While a fish wears shades—who does he see?
A turtle dressed in a straw hat,
Paddles past as he crabs, 'How 'bout that?'

Surfers try to ride the crest,
While waves tease them, quite the jest.
But when they wipe out with a splash,
The beach erupts in laughter's crash.

Mysteries Beneath the Surface

Bubbles pop with secrets shared,
While starfish dance as though they're scared.
A mermaid snorts with salty fries,
Exclaiming, 'What's with all these spies?'

Clams hold meetings, pearls in tow,
Debating whether crabs truly glow.
As fish in ties swim by with flair,
They murmur tales of the sea's wild air.

The Embrace of Coastal Dreams

A crab in a tux, what a sight to see,
He waltzes with waves, so wild and free.
His partner a fish in a shiny gown,
Together they twirl without a frown.

Seagulls in sunhats sing silly songs,
They squawk and they flop, where everyone belongs.
A clam with a drink thinks he's so grand,
While tossing around seashells, oh so unplanned.

Melodies from the Deep Blue

A turtle with shades floats by with a grin,
Singing a tune that makes fish spin.
The starfish clap, but they don't have wrists,
They wiggle along, joining in the twists.

Octopus band in a popping groove,
With eight silly legs, they bust a move.
They tickle the sand, while jellyfish sway,
Making a dance floor out of the bay.

Tranquil Shores at Dusk

A beach ball bounces, straight into the tide,
Where crabs form a team, their pride bona fide.
They cheer on a seagull who's aiming to score,
But the ball goes astray, right to a door.

The sunset's a painter with brushes so bright,
Creating a canvas that feels just right.
Old driftwood laughs, wanting a piece,
Of this whimsical fun, oh wouldn't it cease!

Breezes Carrying Ancient Tales

A parrot in slippers is telling a tale,
Of mermaids on scooters, and fish who sail.
The breeze giggles softly, rustling the breeze,
As crabs knit sweaters from seaweed with ease.

The tide pulls a prank, 'What's lost is now found!'
A flip-flop surfaces, still wet from the ground.
With laughter explosion like bubbles in air,
The shore becomes magic, absurdly rare.

Beyond the Coral's Edge

Fish in bow ties swim with glee,
Eels do the cha-cha, can't you see?
A crab in sunglasses sips his drink,
While a lazy turtle blinks and thinks.

Seashells gossip, they pass the news,
Starfish in flip-flops, having a snooze.
Octopuses juggle coconuts high,
Splashing the pelicans flying by.

Reflections in the Stillness

A dolphin prances, puts on a show,
While a sea cucumber takes it slow.
Under the sun, the jellyfish dance,
Waving their tentacles, taking a chance.

Seagulls trade secrets with cheeky crabs,
Pointing and laughing at all the drabs.
A whale hums tunes from the deep below,
While clams tap their shells to the flow.

The Call of the Untamed Seas

Waves crash like laughter in wild delight,
A pelican named Pete is quite the sight.
He tries on a hat, but it flies away,
Chasing it down, he joins in the play.

Turtles in suits debate what to eat,
While minnows do ballet on tiny feet.
A treasure map's lost, a pirate's dismay,
As crabs take selfies, hip-hip-hooray!

Where the Sky Meets the Sea

Clouds wear their hats, oh what a scene,
While seagulls sketch everyone's cuisine.
A windswept breeze tickles the shore,
As sandcastles laugh, "Build us some more!"

A fish tells a joke, starts an underwater gig,
While a shark in a tie plays it big.
Mermaids enjoy a bubble bath race,
And dolphins give high-fives with such grace.

Sky-born Whispers Above the Sea

The clouds giggle as they float,
Telling tales of a leaping goat.
Seagulls dance in a feathery waltz,
As fish below play catch with faults.

Sunshine dips in a prankster's game,
While crabs wear shells like a fancy name.
A dolphin winks with a splashy cheer,
As we all laugh, from far and near.

Kisses of the Salt-Drenched Winds

The breeze whispers tales, a cheeky tease,
Of sandy toes and a hive of bees.
Flip-flops fly as the sun bakes bright,
Who knew laughter would take flight?

Squirrels in shades, sipping lemonade,
While bathing suits leave us quite delayed.
The tides play tricks on our beachy fun,
As waves shout, 'Catch me if you can, run!'

Nautical Fables in Sunlight

A wise old turtle spins yarns of yore,
While starfish gossip about the shore.
Mermaids giggle, showing off their scales,
As sailors swap tales of ridiculous fails.

With jellyfish dancing in a funky beat,
And crabs trying on shoes that can't be beat.
The waves clap hands and cheer out loud,
Every slip and trip makes us all proud.

Cherished Moments on Turquoise Waters

The sun drops low, a golden tease,
While ticklish waves brush against our knees.
A beach ball flies, misses its catch,
As a rubber duck sings, 'Let's have a match!'

With flamingos in shades sipping sweet brew,
And fish flipping tails with a wink or two.
Under the palm trees, laughter swells,
Creating a symphony that everyone tells.

Driftwood Dreams

On the shore, a log took flight,
Waving 'hi' to seagulls in delight.
It spun around, a dancer bold,
Whispering tales from days of old.

A crab in a top hat strutted past,
Claiming the driftwood for a cast.
He sat with flair, a toast in hand,
To driftwood dreams in a sandy land.

Sunlit Drift

A sunbeam trips upon the sea,
Chasing shadows, wild and free.
Jellyfish twirl in a jelly dance,
While dolphins giggle at their chance.

The waves, they whisper secrets low,
Of surfboards, sandcastles, and glow.
With seagrass hats upon their heads,
The starfish giggle in their beds.

Lighthouses and Lullabies

A lighthouse sings a goofy tune,
To boats that play beneath the moon.
With beams that wink, it shares a joke,
As foghorns add a silly cloak.

In gentle waves, a fish floats by,
Wearing goggles with a curious eye.
It laughs at sailors who effuse,
About the tale of 'lost shoes'.

Celestial Canopies

Under constellations, crabs convene,
Judging the otters on their routine.
The sea turtles roll, a clumsy crew,
While the moon hangs low, a big cheese too.

Banana peels drift in the tide,
As fish start a carnival ride.
With bubbles and giggles, they all agree,
This night is pure comedy by the sea.

Tidal Whispers

The waves dance like they need a break,
They splashed my sandwich, what a mistake!
A seagull steals my chips with pride,
As I chase it down, my giggles can't hide.

A crab gives me a sidelong glance,
I trip over sand, no chance to prance.
The sun winks at me, a golden tease,
While dolphins laugh, swimming with ease.

Salted Serenades

The beach ball rolls like it's on a quest,
And every dive's a silly test.
My pal screams, 'Watch out for that wave!'
But rolls right in—it's a splashy rave!

The fish tease me with their underwater show,
They giggle at the flops I throw.
I try to surf, but fall with flair,
And land right next to someone's chair!

Whispering Waves

Shells tell secrets as I comb the shore,
I swear I heard one, 'We need more!'
The beach chairs squeak, a comical song,
As I wiggle my toes, it's hard to stay strong.

Sunburnt faces look back at me,
As I slip on sunscreen with a sneeze.
A sandcastle crumbles, a sad little fate,
I shout, 'Hey, don't be so late!'

Echoes of the Deep

The tide pulls back, but not quite fair,
It promised a dance but left me bare.
An octopus waves, does a jig right there,
I get caught in the splash, what a wild affair!

Fins flicker, a fish tells me a jest,
'You call that a dive? You need some rest!'
But I laugh it off as I wade on in,
With waves that swish, where fun begins!

The Serenity of Depths

Fish in tuxedos dance with glee,
A crab plays drums, how funny to see!
Mermaids in pearls, sipping on tea,
While octopi juggle in a small marquee.

Seabirds squawk jokes, with a flap and a dive,
A whale tells a tale that barely survives!
Sea cucumbers chuckle, they wobble and thrive,
As starfish debate who's the best to arrive.

Sands and Secrets

A turtle's a tour guide, slow as can be,
He shows us the beach, where sand turns to spree.
The crabs have a dance-off, oh, what jubilee,
While seagulls take bets on who'll win the key!

Amongst all the shells, there's a bottle of cheer,
Inside, a note says, 'Bring candy and beer!'
The sandcastles stand, full of secrets sincere,
But soon, they collapse—ah, the end is near!

Whispers of the Tides

Waves tell secrets as they crash and they sway,
A clam sings softly, in a shy sort of way.
The beach balls bounce, in a farcical play,
While dolphins wear sunglasses, oh, what a display!

Seashells play poker, it's a shell game of luck,
The seaweed's all tangled, oh, what a yuck!
A fish in a fedora says, "What the pluck!",
While sea urchins giggle, so unabashedly stuck!

Dancing Waves Beneath the Moon

Under the moon, the waves start to jig,
Nemo's in spandex, doing a big dig.
With krill on maracas, they bust out a gig,
While plankton sway gently, feeling quite big!

The dolphins form lines for a conga line craze,
The starfish throw glitter, it's a dazzling phase.
Bubbles are popping, with laughter ablaze,
As sea life rejoices in their wavy maze.

Tidepool Tales

In the tidepool, crabs do dance,
With wiggly tails, they take a chance.
Starfish wearing fancy hats,
Joke around like acrobats.

Gelatinous blobs glide with glee,
Pretending to be rocks, you see.
The sea snails sip a bubbly brew,
While clam shells giggle, 'What's new?'

Boundless Blue

The seagulls squawk their silly songs,
They steal my chips, the greedy throngs.
Fish wear goggles and snorkel gear,
Saying, 'Watch out! The humans are here!'

A whale once splashed, made quite a scene,
Drenched a sunbather, all smeared in cream.
The dolphins chuckled, 'That was a splash!'
While mermaids laughed, 'Let's make a dash!'

Heartstrings of the Coast

A crab composed a love-struck tune,
Singing softly beneath the moon.
But the waves laughed, 'You silly bug,
She's probably here for a big hug!'

Seagulls circling, plotting a prank,
One snagged a sandwich, feeling quite rank.
The beachgoers laughed at the ruckus made,
While umbrella hats nearly lost their shade!

Coral Caress

In the reefs, the fish wear ties,
With bubble-blowing friends, they rise.
A octopus painting its best disguise,
While sea cucumbers moan, 'What a surprise!'

Anemones giggle, swaying in trance,
Inviting the clownfish to join their dance.
The seaweed sways, a long, green tease,
While crabs serve lunch, 'Can I take your fees?'

Song of the Sailor

A sailor once lost his own hat,
He chased it down with a squeaky cat.
The waves laughed hard, the gulls took flight,
While fish below danced with delight.

He sang to the sun, with a wink and a grin,
As jellyfish swayed, doing a spin.
His ship started bouncing, a real wild ride,
While crabs stood back, trying to hide!

Veil of the Sea Breeze

A breeze came by with a ticklish tease,
It wrapped my sandwich with delightful ease.
The seagulls squawked, quite outraged, you see,
As I laughed and munched by the tall palm tree.

What capers unfold by the salty swell,
As flip-flops trip, oh, what a spell!
A sandcastle war with lazy old teens,
Made us giggle like silly machines!

Horizon's Reverie

A sailor dreamed of a treasure chest,
Filled with riches and jokes that were best.
He dove from the boat with a splat and a cheer,
To find rubber ducks and a honking deer!

His compass spun like a whirling top,
While mermaids laughed, saying, "Oh, stop!"
Instead of gold, he found a beach ball,
Bouncing and laughing, he gave it his all!

Lush Tropic Whispers

The palms were gossiping with a soft sway,
About a crab who liked to dance all day.
He wore tiny shoes, quite shiny and bright,
Twisting and turning, what a funny sight!

The waves chimed in with a tinkle and jive,
As fish joined in, feeling quite alive.
A parrot squawked, "Best party in town!"
With giggles and laughs, no reason to frown!

Serene Horizons Await

Upon the shore, a crab did dance,
His sideways moves, a comical prance.
Seagulls squawked, making quite a fuss,
While beachgoers laughed, 'Are we on a bus?'

Waves come crashing, what a loud cheer,
Splashing a tourist, who went for a beer.
Shells like jewels, but some are just rocks,
"A treasure!" she cried, forgetting her socks.

Secrets of the Salty Depths

Diving deep, a fish wears a hat,
He greets a turtle, who's quite the pat.
Together they swim, through bubbles and glee,
In a world where seaweed grows like a tree.

Octopus juggling with pearls in a line,
While dolphins do flips, oh isn't it fine?
But watch out for jelly, they're sneaky, it's true,
They'll tickle your toes, and make you go 'boo!'

A Lullaby of Currents

The breeze whispers soft, like a sleepy old cat,
While a fisherman snoozes, tucked snug in his hat.
A crab steals his bait, thinking it's fun,
And the fisherman wakes, saying, "I'm done!"

Seashells giggle as waves come and go,
With seafoam like bubbles in a wacky show.
A starfish plays tag with a curious snail,
Chasing them both in a slippery trail.

Starlit Shores and Gentle Winds

The night sees the stars twinkling with glee,
As a jellyfish glows, so carefree at sea.
They throw a party, a celestial jam,
With whispers of laughter, a wave of 'clam!'

Breezes are playful, tickling the shore,
A sandcastle prince sighs, 'I need some more!'
But a wave sweeps in, with a comedic swoosh,
Leaving nothing but laughter, in a bubbly hush.

Dances of Shadows on the Sand

The seagulls squawk and strut their stuff,
While crabs in tuxedos say, "That's enough!"
A flip-flop flies, like a rebel in flight,
Landing on sunbathers, oh what a sight!

Sandcastles crumble with each wave's embrace,
The tide giggles, splashing all over the place.
A child yells, 'Mom! I made seafood today!'
With a bucket of shells and a starfish array!

Beach balls are bouncing like they've gone mad,
While teeny ghosts chase them, oh aren't they glad?
In this sandy stage, the silliness reigns,
As laughter entwines with the sunshine's bright chains.

The Gift of Diamonds on the Waves

A glittery splash lands right on my toes,
I scream like a dolphin, my squeals overflow.
The fish throw a party — they're dressed in fine gear,
While mermaids giggle, oh what a cheer!

A crab with a crown plots a royal escape,
He's a king of the beach, in his own bumpy shape.
He shimmies past seashells all shiny and bright,
Saying, 'Who needs a throne, when the sand feels just right?'

The waves wrap gifts, like a child's wild dream,
With treasures of foam in a white frothy gleam.
So grab your sunhat and dance on this spree,
For being this silly is always the key!

Horizon Scents and Salted Caramel

The breeze whiffs a scent like popcorn and fun,
It's a salty delight under the bright golden sun.
But alas, there's a seagull who thinks it's his snack,
He swoops down with a crunch, leaving nothing intact!

A picnic blanket flaps like a kite on a spree,
While ants gather crumbs like it's their jubilee.
We dine on delights, a feast for the ages,
While sand tickles toes, like a page full of pages.

The sun sets on laughter, the waves dance in cheer,
With flavors of caramel lingering near.
As friends swap tall tales with a wink and a grin,
Our sandy adventures are where laughs begin!

Chasing Tidal Pools at Sunset

A wobbly octopus shows off his flair,
While sea stars play games without any care.
The sunset wraps colors like a warm, cozy quilt,
As we race over rocks, oh what fun we've built!

In tidal pools splash, where little fish dart,
A shrimp joins the chase — he's got quite the heart!
We giggle and dance, in this watery maze,
Creating new stories that's sure to amaze.

But wait! What's this? A sock in the tide!
An old shoe joins in, it's a clam's new ride.
With treasure and laughter, we'll splash 'til it's dark,
Chasing our shadows, just look for the spark!

Shores of Mystery and Magic

In a land where coconuts grow,
I found a crab stealing my shoe.
He looked quite smug, a master of stealth,
Sipping a drink, calling it health.

Seagulls squawking at clever tricks,
Dancing on waves like playful bricks.
I tried to join, but fell on my face,
The joy of the beach—a comical chase.

A flip-flop fight with a foam-topped wave,
The salt and the laughter are hard to save.
With every splash, a chuckle erupts,
In the land where the funny fish jumps.

As twilight stirs the horizon's hues,
I ponder the sea and its silly muse.
A mermaid winks from her watery den,
Inviting me back to the fun again.

Breath of the Briny Wind

The wind whispers tales of lagging fools,
Who took their boats onto the wrong pools.
With sails that flapped like panicked flocks,
They danced to tunes of the ticking clocks.

Breezes blow with a cheeky grin,
While I search for where the fun begins.
A dolphin laughs as it flips around,
In this breezy realm, silly joy is found.

Fishing for laughter with a net of jokes,
Retrieving smiles instead of the flokes.
Every catch brings a tickle or two,
Oh, the salty breeze knows how to renew.

With a gust that promises tricks and cheer,
I clutch my hat as the sails appear.
The briny breaths of fun are here,
Too precious to waste, so let's commandeer!

The Soliloquy of Sailors

A sailor sings a funny yelp,
As he wrestles with his own kelp.
It tangles his legs in a slippery dance,
His mates roll with laughter, not a second glance.

The compass spins with a quirky glee,
Leading them all to a giant pea.
They anchor down to feast and play,
Trading tales of the wacky day.

A parrot squawks, mocking their plight,
Squawking "Land ho!" in the midst of night.
With every riddle from the stars above,
These sailors laugh struck by the tides of love.

As sea creatures join in the banter so vast,
Even the moon laughs, forgetting the past.
They toast with coconuts under the sun,
In the breezy world where the jokes are spun.

Twilight Reflections on Salted Skin

The sun dips down with a chuckling sigh,
As I chase the shadows, oh my, oh my!
Salted skin glistens, reflecting the fun,
With every wave, I'm kissed by the sun.

Jellyfish jiggle as the tide comes in,
I dance with them, what a silly spin!
Regretted my moves as I tripped on the sand,
But laughter erupts—it's all just grand!

Fireflies flicker with a twinkling cheer,
They whisper secrets for every ear.
As the night deepens, the hilarity flows,
In this coastal haven, silliness glows.

With a drink in hand and laughter to spare,
We toast to the moments, the joys we share.
Twilight giggles wrap us tenderly,
In a world where the funny runs wild and free.

Whispers in the Dune Grasses

Beneath the sun, the sand does sway,
A crab performs a dance ballet.
Seagulls gossip, quite the chat,
While I slip sideways to avoid that!

The lizards laugh in sunlit glee,
As I trip over my own two feet.
A tumble here, a stumble there,
The surf's my friend, but oh, beware!

Flip-flops flying, sunburned nose,
I chase my hat as the warm wind blows.
The dunes are whispering secret tales,
Of clumsy tourists and their fails!

Yet laughter reigns, as splashes fly,
I splash my pals, and they just sigh.
With goofy grins, we dance and play,
Creating memories in a fun-filled way!

Sheltering in the Shade of Palms

Beneath the fronds, I hide away,
As squirrels plot their nutty play.
The breeze delivers whispers bright,
While I perfect my sunbathing sight.

A coconut falls with a clunk and roll,
Cracking open my peaceful stroll.
The monkeys laugh, a cheeky crew,
With sticky fingers, they grab my brew!

The hammock squeaks, like it's in on a joke,
As my snacks are swiped, and I just choke.
The sun beams down, I start to fry,
While palms wave softly, oh my, oh my!

Yet all around, the world finds cheer,
With laughter echoing, sweet and clear.
In shaded nooks, we share a grin,
Life's lighter wrapped in tropical skin!

Catching the Wind with Open Arms

Setting sail with a laugh today,
The wind told me, "Come out and play!"
The sailboat tilts amidst the fun,
I'm trying my best, but I've come undone!

The seagulls sneak and steal my fries,
I toss them crumbs, much to my surprise!
A dolphin jumps, a splash, a twist,
I laugh so hard, can't resist!

Yet tangled lines and hats blown far,
Create a show, oh, what bizarre!
The sun shines down, and life feels grand,
As I cling tight with one goofy hand!

With every gust, my giggles rise,
In salty air, I hear the skies.
Life's a riot upon the waves,
And I'm the jester that it braves!

A Sailor's Hut in the Breezy Bay

In a hut with walls that sway and creak,
I chase my dreams and feel unique.
The wind plays music on my door,
While I try to dance, and trip on the floor!

My fishing line's a tangled mess,
A fish swims by with no interest.
Yet here I sit, with ice-cold drink,
In this wacky life, I can't help but wink!

Pelicans dive as I munch on snacks,
They eye my chips, and my sanity cracks.
With cheesy grins, I share with glee,
Those feathered friends, they're pals, you see?

So here's to huts, to laughs, to play,
And all the silliness of the day.
As waves come rolling in with flair,
I raise my glass to the salty air!

Invocations to the Sea Goddess

Oh, sea lady with hair of kelp,
Please grant us a wave or two,
We promise not to use your shell,
For we're quite content with the view.

We bring you offerings of sand,
And donuts that float on the tide,
Just don't use our sunscreen, so tanned,
Or we might have to run and hide.

With seagulls as our singing friends,
We'll dance on the beach till the night,
Just make sure our flip-flops don't end,
In the depths of your watery sight.

So bless us with ripples and fun,
And laughter that echoes with glee,
For here we'll enjoy in the sun,
Oh, grant us your whimsy at sea.

The Palette of Seafoam and Sun

The hues of the shore, so sublime,
With ice cream that melts in the heat,
We mix all our flavors in rhyme,
While beach balls bounce under our feet.

Dive into the splash, we'll all cheer,
The seagulls eyeing our fries with glee,
With water so salty, never fear,
The crabs dance around in the spree.

Our towels are speckled with sand,
As we stroll with our shades on our eyes,
We gather in cliques, a grand band,
And fashion our crowns made of fries.

So let's dip our toes in the waves,
And wrestle with clouds made of fluff,
With giggles that echo like braves,
We'll paint our own canvas of stuff.

Castaways on a Canvas of Blue

We're marooned on our sunny land,
With coconuts as our best pals,
The fish hold a party so grand,
While we juggle seashells and gals.

Our sailboat's made out of flip-flops,
Oh, how we'll drift on this breeze,
Let's toast to our tropical stops,
With smoothies as thick as the trees.

We've drawn treasure maps in the sand,
With X marks the spot of our chips,
For seasickness comes close at hand,
When the seagulls come for our dips.

So here's to our castaway days,
With laughter that rises like tide,
In sunglasses and silly charades,
We'll conquer the waves with our pride.

Whispered Secrets of the Aquatic Realm

The fish have a party beneath,
Where seaweed shakes and waves wiggle,
They whisper their secrets in breath,
While we try not to smirk or giggle.

With turtles who wear funky hats,
And crabs with their soapy attire,
We join in their laughter and chats,
As dolphins unload their fun fire.

The clams have a gossiping spree,
While octopus plays hide-and-seek,
Their stories are bizarre but free,
We're rolling with laughter, not meek.

So come join this buoyant brigade,
In the giggles of bubbles and foam,
With secrets that never will fade,
We'll frolic and dance in our home.

Poetry of the Surf and Shore

The gulls are loud, they squawk and dive,
They think they own the beach, alive!
My sandwich flies to take a ride,
As I chase it down, my pride has died.

The waves crash down, a messy splash,
I try to surf, but oh, I crash!
The board's my foe, it spins and twirls,
I bob like plankton, oh, what a whirl!

Flip-flops missing, lost in sand,
A treasure hunt, oh, isn't it grand?
I slip and slide on seaweed slick,
Laughing at my own clumsy trick.

The sun is hot, I feel like fry,
A lightly toasted human pie.
But with each wave, I rise and fall,
In this wild game, I'm having a ball!

Eden's Buffeted Sanctuary

The palm trees sway with lots of flair,
It's like they're dancing, without a care.
A coconut lands, I duck and weave,
I swear that tree's out to deceive!

The sand's too hot, I hop and prance,
In flip-flops, oh, I take my chance.
Bare feet now hot, like molten cheese,
I dance around with awkward ease.

Crabs in the sand doing a jig,
I join them too, feeling quite big.
But just like that, I lose my grip,
I tumble down—a comical flip!

Seagulls are eyeing my tasty snack,
One grabs a chip, and that's a fact!
Laughter echoes under the sun,
In Eden's care, we all have fun!

Underneath the Waves' Spell

Dive on in, the water's fine,
But here comes a wave, it's not divine!
I splash around, just like a seal,
With grace like this, how can I feel?

A snorkeling mask, all fogged and glued,
I can't see fish; that's just plain rude!
I bump a rock, I screech and shout,
A fish just giggled—what's that about?

Bubbles rise up like little friends,
They float away, and soon it ends.
I wave goodbye, with a silly grin,
Who knew the depths held such a spin?

Out of breath, I find the shore,
My legs are jelly, what a chore!
But with a splash, and a hearty cheer,
I'll dive again, my friends, never fear!

Tempest and Tranquility

Storm clouds brewing, a sight to see,
I hold my hat, it's almost free!
The wind howls loud, a scary sound,
Who knew our fun could spin around?

The waves are dancing, tossing high,
I hold my drink, it's do or die!
A rogue wave crashes, I spill my fizzy,
The fish all giggle, and it feels dizzy.

But in the calm, once storms have passed,
We find sweet laughter, joys amassed.
With sunlit waves, we reignite,
Celebrating silly, what pure delight!

So here we sail, 'twixt wild and mild,
Life's a beach, oh, so beguiled!
Let's dance with waves, both loud and meek,
In every splash, we cheekily speak!

Secrets of the Blue

A fish wore a hat, quite out of place,
He danced with a crab, both made a face.
A dolphin named Fred, with a wink and a grin,
Said, "Join us for drinks, but don't let fish in!"

They held a grand feast on a big, sunny rock,
With seaweed spaghetti, a slippery shock.
The octopus juggled while seagulls all cheered,
As shells clinked together, not one salty tear!

A clam shared a tale, but no one believed,
About treasure and gold, yet no one got deceived.
A sea lion cracked jokes, oh, they laughed till they cried,
While waves whispered secrets that swirled with the tide.

The party wrapped up as the sun dipped out,
With fishy confetti and a great big shout.
So remember this tale of the funny fish crew,
There's magic afoot in the deep shades of blue!

Breeze-Kissed Isles

On the shore a coconut hat took a leap,
To join a wild dance where the crabs formed a sweep.
They twirled in the sand, what a curious sight,
With a breeze as their partner, they danced through the night.

A parrot with style, in shades oh-so-bright,
Said, "Get your salsa moves, it's time to ignite!"
The starfish in sandals looked quite out of place,
But shook to the rhythm, no sense of disgrace.

The sea turtle waddled, looking quite cool,
While jellyfish floated—now that was a school!
They made quite the scene, with laughter and cheer,
As waves played along, whispering humor quite near.

So next time you wander where breezes delight,
Remember those critters and dance through the night.
For in every soft breeze, there's laughter, you see,
On those whimsically fun, breeze-kissed isles of glee!

Embrace of the Sea

The seagull was doing the cha-cha quite bold,
While barnacles giggled, they loved the unfold.
A hermit crab villain, with mischief in eyes,
Stole shells left behind, oh, what a surprise!

The seaweed all fluffed into hairstyles so wild,
As anemones pouted and beauty was styled.
"Just look at my flair!" said a fish with a grin,
"The tides may be rough, but this party's a win!"

They sang all their tales of beach life and strife,
Of waves that would crash, and the joy of fish life.
An octopus whispered, "These moments are free,
So let's raise a fin to the embrace of the sea!"

As dusk settled in, the stars jumped alive,
With jokes shared as treasures, the laughter would thrive.
So if you're feeling dull, just take a drive,
To where the waves tumble, come dance and revive!

Lullabies of the Nautilus

A nautilus swayed to a tune from below,
With soft lullabies that made sea critters glow.
He hummed to the shells; they echoed in cheer,
While clam shells conspired, and giggled in fear.

With tides that would chuckle and bubbles that play,
They tucked in their dreams at the end of the day.
The flounders all yawned, tucking fins in tight,
As a whale softly crooned, what a sleepy sight!

The seahorses swayed gently, like leaves on a breeze,
Cuddled up close, oh, the comfort in seas.
Each wink of a star was a wink at the fun,
As waves rocked them softly, the day's work was done.

So drift into dreams where the sea offers grace,
In the arms of the deep, find your cozy new place.
For with lullabies swirling, and joy in each sound,
You'll wake with a smile when the sun's shining round!

A Journey to Hidden Atolls

We sailed on a boat made of spare parts,
With sandwiches packed, our adventurous hearts.
The fish wore sunglasses, swimming with glee,
While crabs held a conga on the sun-kissed spree.

The sun was a pancake, round and so warm,
But seagulls swooped down, alarmed by our charm.
They squawked like old ladies, gossiping loud,
As we danced on the deck, feeling oh so proud.

A dolphin showed off with flips in the air,
We cheered and we laughed—did he stop to care?
A pirate's old treasure, some junk on the shore,
It turned out to be flip-flops: oh, what a bore!

Yet laughter rang out, carried on the breeze,
A day full of blunders, oh, with such ease.
Shiny shells jived, they joined in our jest,
As we ended our trip, feeling truly blessed.

Tidal Dances Under Mango Trees

The waves took a leap, just like my best friend,
Who tripped on a sand dune that would not pretend.
We hollered with laughter, oh what a sight,
While a crab took a bow, thinking it was right.

Mangoes were ripe, a feast in the shade,
We threw them like Frisbees, what a game we made!
The juice dripped and splattered, like art gone awry,
As bees formed a buzz, watching us fly.

A toucan told jokes from a low-hanging branch,
While my friend made a smoothie—a very bad chance.
The blender revolved like a rollercoaster ride,
And soon it was pouring down, oh what a slide!

The laughter erupted, filling the air,
With dancing and munching, we had not a care.
The sun set in colors, an artist's delight,
And we wrapped up the day, feeling so light.

Skimming Stones, Catching Stars

We gathered our pebbles, all shiny and round,
Planning to skim them, with joy all around.
But half hit the water, while the rest hit our toes,
Resulting in squeals, well, nobody knows!

The stars on the beach looked like tiny stray friends,
While we bobbed and we weaved, on the sand without ends.
My friend tried to catch one, tripped over a mound,
And fell in the waves, but still laughed all around.

A seagull flew over, with a wink in its eye,
Maybe it judged us, oh what a sly guy!
We sent out a challenge, we'd skim with finesse,
Only to find out our skills were a mess!

But the giggles and splashes, they echoed so clear,
A reminder that joy is the best souvenir.
With pebbles as trophies, and laughter aglow,
We conquered the night, with a whimsical show.

Beneath the Swell of Blue Horizons

We set out on journey, our spirits so high,
With dreams of wild turtles, beneath the wide sky.
But dolphins played tricks, sneaking into our feast,
They swirled and they twirled, the cleverest beast!

The sun wore a hat, it seemed quite absurd,
While the waves giggled loudly, not one single word.
"Grab the sunscreen!" yelled Sam, "I'm turning to toast!"

As a crab eyed our chips, he was quite the bold host.

The waves whispered secrets, we couldn't quite catch,
A fish in a tuxedo, oh, what a match!
It danced on the surface, with elegance grand,
While we dropped our snacks—did it think that was planned?

Our hearts overflowed, like a bucket with glee,
With went home with stories, from the sun-kissed spree.
A toast to the quirks, oh, what a delight—
For laughter and sunshine can brighten the night.

The Dance of Distant Shores

The seagulls squawk with glee,
They steal my sandwich with such ease.
While beach balls bounce and twirl,
Kids laugh, as waves unfurl.

A crab in sunglasses struts about,
In flip-flops, he shows off, and shouts.
He dances wildly on the sand,
Drawing a crowd, it's quite a band!

With jellyfish playing hide and seek,
I ask them questions, but they're too meek.
Starfish wink from their rocky beds,
As I trip over my own two legs.

So grab a towel, join the fun,
The sun is out; let's make a run!
With laughter echoing in the air,
Life's a party—oh, don't you dare!

Currents of Tomorrow

The surfboard slipped from my grasp,
I yelped loud, was gone in a gasp.
The waves giggled as I went down,
Emerging, I wore seaweed like a crown.

A fish in shades passed me by,
I swear I heard it sigh.
"Take a dip, you wobbly dude,"
But all I could do was brood.

With mermaids grinning, they tease,
"When's the last time you've seen your knees?"
I try to swim, but oh, what a sight,
Flopping around, it's pure delight!

So here's to the splash, a weekly score,
Let's raise a glass, to the beach encore!
With each wave, a giggly fight,
Tomorrow's recall will be outta sight!

Untamed Horizons

A parrot squawks, "Hey, land a hand!"
While I try to build my dream sand land.
It topples over—oh, what a mess!
Now it's a moat, I guess—no less!

A dolphin jumps, flipping with flair,
I clap excitedly, losing my hair.
It takes my hat with a cheeky splash,
In pursuit, I take off, oh what a dash!

With pineapples dancing on the grill,
I attempt a hula, giving a thrill.
The locals chuckle, offering a drink,
"Stay wild, my friend, don't ever think!"

So let's toast to sun and silly fights,
To mischief that fills our sunny nights.
With laughter forever in sight,
We embrace the joy, so outta sight!

Moonlit Refuge

The moon is high, and here they come,
Lost flip-flops marching, looking glum.
They form a line, a sassy parade,
Giggling softly under the shade.

Crabs in suits, all dressed to impress,
Hold evening soirées, what a mess!
A dance-off starts 'twixt starfish and me,
Who knew crustaceans could dance so free?

Tide pools giggle, reflecting the sky,
As I trip on shells and let out a cry.
"Don't be shy, it's just a stumble,"
The slippery rocks say, as I tumble.

With a sigh of joy, I bask in this,
A night full of laughter, oh bliss!
Under the stars, let's laugh some more,
Tomorrow brings tides for laughs galore!

Navigation through Reflection's Glow

I sailed with a rubber duck, oh what a sight,
It quacked in the day and sang in the night.
With a map made of pizza, we charted our way,
To the land of lost socks—what a silly play!

The compass flipped sideways, lost in the fun,
Pointing to beaches where everyone runs.
A crab wearing sunglasses, full of such flair,
Directed our laughter, without a care!

Conch Shells and the Music of the Sea

A conch shell tells tales of sailors so brave,
But mostly, it whispers of a sandy rave.
With hermit crabs dancing, the beat was just right,
Making moonwalks in shells—they did it all night!

Seagulls were singing, off-key yet bold,
Trading old gossip of treasures untold.
The tides rolled in laughter and splashed on the shore,
As fish started twerking—who knew? There's more!

Light as Air on a Coastal Breeze

The wind blew my hat right into a tree,
It whispered, "Catch me!" like it's funny and free.
With a leap and a twirl, I danced with the breeze,
Trying to snag it, but giggling with ease.

A seagull swooped down for a nibble or two,
Popping my picnic—what a feathery crew!
Sand castled dreams washed away with the tide,
Making silly formless sculptures we'd ride!

Seashell Monologues at Sunrise

At dawn, seashells gathered for a witty debate,
Arguing who's luckier with a sunniest fate.
One claimed to have seen a dolphin in flight,
While the other just snored—no dramatic insight!

They jostled for space on the warm early sands,
Swapping tall tales with exaggerated hands.
With bubbles of laughter, they echoed their tales,
As crabs rolled their eyes—oh, what silly trails!

A Parade of Winds in the Bay

A gust came in, all dressed in white,
Twisting my hat, oh what a sight!
Then back it swirled, a playful tease,
As seagulls laughed, riding the breeze.

The sails were up, but boats went down,
Caught in the whirl of that rogue clown.
With waves that giggled, splashed and spun,
It seemed Old Man Wind was having fun!

A crab waved goodbye, snappy and quick,
While jellyfish danced, oh what a trick!
They frolicked together in deep sea glee,
A party unleashed upon the sea!

As I watched, my drink took a dive,
My umbrella hid, no chance to survive.
With chuckles all round, a tidal ballet,
The winds had declared: it's time to play!

Musings in the Misty Morning

Fog rolled in like a fluffy thief,
Where's my coffee? Oh, what a grief!
The sun peeked out with a shy hello,
But mist just giggled, refusing to go.

A sailor yawned, lost in his dreams,
Thought he saw fish with glittering gleams.
But it was just seagulls wearing hats,
Trading their tales with friendly chats.

The tides had plans, you could bet your boots,
Spinning their tales with laughs and hoots.
While crabs shared secrets beneath the brine,
In a morning mist that felt divine.

With a splash and a wink, the day awoke,
Turning the fog into wisps of smoke.
And as the laughter echoed anew,
I raised my cup for a toast or two!

Above the Reef's Rhapsody

Corals trumpet, in colors so bright,
Fish in tuxedos, oh what a sight!
They jive and they wiggle, in perfect sync,
While turtles slow dance, what do you think?

A clownfish honked, trying to compete,
But his act was more a floundering feat.
The starfish rolled their eyes with grace,
"Is this a show or a clumsy race?"

The bubbles chuckled as they made their way,
Pop, pop, pop! They joined the fray.
And somewhere a dolphin, with style and flair,
Gave a flip in the air, with utmost care.

In this underwater, comedic scene,
Where laughter echoed, and joy was keen.
As the reef buzzed on with zest and zeal,
I couldn't help but feel the appeal!

The Allure of Distant Shores

A ship sailed off, with dreams in tow,
Decks filled with treats, oh-so-slow!
But the compass twirled, in a comical spin,
As Captain Jack grinned with a mischievous grin.

Tropical maps turned into jokes,
With islands like pancakes, made of folks!
A parrot squawked, "Let's flip to the left!"
While all the crew just giggled and heft.

With every wave, a story's told,
Of treasure and tales, both brave and bold.
Mistakes made in laughter, with every trip,
As beaches beckon for a frosty sip.

So let's toast to travels, wild and free,
To the mischief of winds and salty glee.
For every distant shore has charms galore,
And laughter awaits, evermore!

Horizon Dreams in Soft Sand

Seagulls squawk, they steal my fries,
With their beady little eyes.
I sunbathe while I'm covered in cream,
Must look like a giant ice cream dream.

Kids laugh, they're running around,
Building castles on the ground.
A wave crashes, they give a squeal,
Their fortress gone—it's just unreal!

My flip-flops flop, I trip and fall,
I blame the sand for all my sprawls.
The beach umbrella decides to flee,
As if it longs for the rolling sea.

The sky turns pink; it's time for chow,
Some greasy fish—oh, take a bow!
I look to my left, to my right,
And see my snacks all take flight!

Colors of Corals and Calm

I dived down deep, what did I find?
A wiggly fish, he looked quite blind.
With polka dots and stripes galore,
He swam past me, I yelled, "Hey, more!"

Oh, look at the colors, so bright, so loud,
Underwater disco, man, I was proud.
My snorkel's leaking, I start to choke,
I rise to the top, just like a joke!

A crab scuttles by with a sassy stride,
I swear he winked—what a wild ride!
The reef choir sings off-key to the sun,
I bop with the fish—it's all in good fun!

A sea turtle glides like a lazy old chap,
"Get a move on!" I laugh, give him a clap.
We're here for a dance and a twirl or two,
But I'm really just craving a burger with goo!

A Fisherman's Tale of the Deep

Old Frank claims he caught a fish,
It sparkled and danced, fulfilled his wish.
But halfway home, it vanished away,
He swears a dolphin snatched it that day!

With bait and tackle, he casts his line,
While I sip soda and munch on a pine.
"Any luck?" I yell; he just grins and grumps,
The only things biting are his trusty pumps!

He tells tales of sharks, oh, they were grand,
He flexes his muscles—he's lost in the sand.
"I battled the waves, I braved the storm,"
But he looks more like a fish stick, all warm!

He pulls in a net, what's there to see?
A rubber boot, a can, and a seaweed spree.
"Behold my catch!" he winks with glee,
Frank's fishing tales—just comedy!

Echoes of the Pelagic Symphony

The whales are singing, oh what a tune,
They crack jokes with the stars and the moon.
Their bubbles rise like laughter in air,
I dance on the shore without a care.

Dolphins darting, a game of tag,
I try to join, but my legs just lag.
They giggle and jump, doing flips with grace,
While I trip over sand, what a silly race!

Sea turtles shout, "This party's grand!"
While I sip coconut from a plastic hand.
The conch shells boast tales of the past,
But I'm too busy munching a snack that's vast!

The tides change rhythms, the currents sway,
I hear the foam whisper, "Come out and play!"
With laughter and waves, a magical scene,
Where nature sings, and I feel like a queen!

Paradise Beneath the Palm Canopy

Underneath the leaves so green,
I found a crab doing the cha-cha scene.
He twirled and danced with much delight,
While seagulls cheered; what a funny sight!

Coconuts fell with a thud and a cheer,
I leaped to catch one, but no luck, I fear!
A squirrel snickered from a nearby tree,
As I stumbled, oh woe, why not just flee?

The sun did shine like a spotlight's beam,
I built a sandcastle; it was a dream!
But waves rushed in with a sneaky plan,
And my fortress sank—oh, that crafty man!

With flip-flops on, I made my retreat,
Chasing a crab that danced on my feet,
We laughed as we waddled along the shore,
Who knew a day could bring so much more?

The Rhythm of Faraway Islands

On a distant shore that's oh so bright,
I spotted a parrot taking flight.
He squawked a tune, offbeat and loud,
While fish swam by with a wiggly crowd.

The waves made music—a bubbly sound,
As I tried to dance but fell on the ground.
A starfish chuckled, jiggled with glee,
Said, 'Join the party; it's all about me!'

With a bucket hat and sunscreen galore,
I strutted around, quite ready to score.
But my towel blew away, a snatchy thief,
And the crab waved goodbye; oh, what a grief!

Seashells held secrets, laughter galore,
As waves kept crashing, begging for more.
With a splash and a grin, my day took a twist,
Dancing with critters on nature's own list!

Gossamer Dreams on the Coast

Dreams float by like clouds in the sky,
While jellyfish jive, they make me sigh.
They glow in the dark with a shimmering dance,
I tried once to join, but ruined my chance!

The breeze carried whispers, oh what a tease,
As I chased my hat, soaring with ease.
A pelican laughed while stealing my fries,
I'm starting to think he's the king in disguise!

With buckets and shovels, we built a great wall,
But a rogue wave came, it took us to fall.
Flopping like fish, we stumbled with grace,
As the tide rolled in, oh what a race!

Under the sun, my friends danced around,
While sand got stuck in places profound.
We giggled and twirled, with spirits set free,
Who knew shore adventures could be so zany?

French Toast on a Tropical Island

Sipping coconuts, what a delight,
I ordered toast but it's a weird sight.
The chef wore shades and a grass skirt too,
Flipping French toast while hula-ing, woo!

With syrup rivers flowing down the plate,
I took a big bite; now, is this fate?
A parrot swooped down, aiming to share,
But missed the toast; better luck in the air!

The sun was bright, I felt so alive,
As ants marched by in a foodie drive.
They fancied the crumbs, oh what a feast,
While I chased them off, feeling like a beast!

So here on the shore, I laugh with a cheer,
For toast on the sand is worth every smirk.
A fruity cocktail and laughter abounds,
This island life is where joy truly sounds!

Echoes of Marine Serenades

The fish threw a party, but no one could swim,
They danced like they had legs, looking quite grim.
Jellyfish did the limbo, oh what a sight,
While seagulls squawked tunes, from morning till night.

A crab in a tux, thought he was so grand,
But slipped on some seaweed and fell in the sand.
The shells held their laughter, they couldn't keep still,
While dolphins played DJ, oh what a thrill!

A whale made a splash with a flap and a flip,
The mermaids joined in, taking quite a trip.
They twirled with the tides, in a waltz with the breeze,
While turtles joined hands, saying, "Aren't we a tease?"

So if you hear laughter, just listen real close,
It's the sea having fun, we're all just its host!
With bubbles and glee, and a surfboard or two,
Join in on the humor, come on, join the crew!

Sun-Kissed Sand and Driftwood

On a beach made of candy, a crab wore a hat,
He danced with a seagull, a curious brat.
Their shadows stretched long like a game of charades,
While waves cheered them on, in playful cascades.

A driftwood named Chester, oh what a wise guy,
Told tales of the sea, while seabirds flew by.
He claimed he once surfed on a log shaped like cheese,
And caught a tall wave with deceptive ease.

The sun hired a kite, to brighten the day,
But it swooped too low and got tangled in play.
Now they soar hand in hand, with laughter so bright,
Creating a spectacle, oh what a sight!

With shells as sweet spoons, they feasted on sand,
While crabs did the cha-cha, all hand in hand.
Next time you wander where the sun loves to bake,
Remember the humor that sea critters make!

Lighthouses Guarding the Night

A lighthouse stood tall, with a wink in its light,
Telling jokes to the ships, keeping spirits so bright.
It said, "Watch your course, don't bump into me!",
As boats laughed and dashed, like they were carefree.

The moon joined the fun, wearing shades of pure gold,
While stars scattered sparkles, so daring and bold.
A pelican, dressed as a captain so grand,
Took charge of the deck with a wave of his hand.

The waves cracked up jokes that were cheesy, no doubt,
While fishermen chuckled, as they tossed lines about.
The lighthouse just smiled, with its beacon's warm glow,
Saying, "Stay in your lane, just follow the flow!"

At night, it would sing to the fishes below,
"Stop flopping around, let's enjoy the show!"
With laughter as bright as the stars in the skies,
The ocean embraced all with hilarious ties!

The Colors of a Twilight Cascade

At dusk, the sky painted with pinks and with blues,
Seashells wearing sunglasses, catching a snooze.
The crabs on the shore, playing hide-and-seek,
While otters just giggled, oh how they would squeak!

A starfish contemplated its future career,
As a sponge diver, surely - that's premier!
With dreams of donning a little cap and a vest,
But first had to master the floating, the best!

As twilight wrapped gently around all the sea,
A seal cracked a joke, with a glee of esprit.
"Why did the fish blush?" it asked with a grin,
"Because it saw the ocean's depths, and got a fin!"

Now fireflies lit up in a dance with delight,
As waves sang the finale of a thrilling night.
So next time you glimpse at the sky's mystique,
Remember the laughter that's meant to be chic!

Ripples of Forgotten Stories

Once a fish told a joke, quite strange,
It swam 'round the reef, felt a bit deranged.
A crab heard the punchline and snapped with glee,
While a seal rolled over, laughing at the sea.

The octopus winked, with eight arms in play,
Said, 'I got my own tales—guess what? They're all cray!'
A dolphin chimed in, 'Let's not forget fun,
The squid's got a secret, that's second to none.'

Starfish on duty roll their eyes in jest,
Saying, 'We're just here, taking a sunbathing rest.'
But soon they'll be gossiping out on the rocks,
About all the antics of sneaky old fox.

Just dock your worries, let laughter unfold,
In this realm of silliness, behold and behold.
There's never a dull day in blue hues and glows,
With ripples of humor where the laughter flows.

Skylines Across Endless Waters

The seagulls are squawking about the new trend,
'Why wear a hat when you can just bend?'
With winds that are wild and freedom so near,
They'll sing fashion's praises while sipping on beer.

Meanwhile, a pelican's fishing, quite sleek,
Dropping his lunch—a rare gourmet leak.
He dives with a flourish, but oh, what a blunder,
Now he's stuck with a crab that likes to throw thunder.

Across the blue waves, a boat drifts by,
With musicians on board singing songs that defy.
'A fish stole my pick, now I'm corralled in a tune,'
They laugh 'til the dolphins come dancing at noon.

So cherish the skyline, where fun meets the sun,
With laughter and waves, life's never done.
A melody echoes, laughter's the chief,
As seabirds all dance, giving humor its reef.'

Sailboats and Starry Nights

Under a blanket of twinkling bright stars,
A sailboat sways gently, entertains Mars.
A raccoon on board, he thinks he's quite sly,
Stealing snacks from the crew with a mischievous eye.

The captain is snoring, oh, what a loud sound,
While a cat's eyeing fish, on deck she's quite found.
The gulls swoop in, plot a heist on the bait,
But conveniently forget it's already too late.

As laughter erupts from a joke told on deck,
'Why doesn't the shark ever play check?'
The answer's still floating, lost in the breeze,
As sailors all giggle and snack with such ease.

For under the stars, where the silliness roams,
Each wave brings a tale, in this voyage of homes.
So, pull out the sails, let the fun take its flight,
With laughter as compass, we sail through the night.

Nature's Brush on Ivory Shores

With paints made of sunsets, the beach has a plan,
To dress itself up like a beachside fan.
A crab strolls by, with a tiny beret,
Saying, 'I'm ready for fashion, it's my kind of day!'

The tides wash up treasures, shells gleam at dawn,
Sprinkling pure madness, like confetti of yawn.
A child creates castles that shape sounds in sand,
While a dog spies a seagull, oh, how they'll stand!

Each wave's a new drip in this masterpiece bright,
Colors merging, dancing, from morning to night.
With laughter erupting from feet in the foam,
It's a gallery of giggles, in nature's fine home.

So grab your own bucket, and roll up your sleeves,
Join in the art where the funny stuff weaves.
With brushes made of joy, on shores ivory kissed,
It's a day to remember, how can we resist?

www.ingramcontent.com/pod-product-compliance
Lightning Source LLC
Chambersburg PA
CBHW072216070526
44585CB00015B/1357